WHY NEWS
MATTERS

FREE PRESS
CORNERSTONE
OF DEMOCRACY

BY DUCHESS HARRIS, JD, PHD

Core Library

An Imprint of Abdo Publishing
abdopublishing.com

Cover image: Freedom of the press is guaranteed by
the First Amendment.

abdopublishing.com

Published by Abdo Publishing, a division of ABDO, PO Box 398166, Minneapolis, Minnesota 55439. Copyright © 2018 by Abdo Consulting Group, Inc. International copyrights reserved in all countries. No part of this book may be reproduced in any form without written permission from the publisher. Core Library™ is a trademark and logo of Abdo Publishing.

Printed in the United States of America, North Mankato, Minnesota
102017
012018

Cover Photo: Rainmaker Photo/MediaPunch/IPX/AP Images
Interior Photos: Rainmaker Photo/MediaPunch/IPX/AP Images, 1; Everett Collection Historical/Alamy, 4–5; Bettmann/Getty Images, 9; Nati Harnik/AP Images, 11; Jim Beckel/The Oklahoman/AP Images, 14–15; Red Line Editorial, 17, 35; AP Images, 19; Library of Congress, 22–23; Stock Montage/Archive Photos/Getty Images, 26, 43; Harris & Ewing Collection/Library of Congress, 28; Ken Feil/The Washington Post/Getty Images, 30–31; The Washington Post/Getty Images, 34; Kyodo/AP Images, 36; Erkan Avci/Anadolu Agency/Getty Images, 38–39

Editor: Patrick Donnelly
Imprint Designer: Maggie Villaume
Series Design Direction: Megan Anderson
Contributor: Amy C. Rea

Publisher's Cataloging-in-Publication Data

Names: Harris, Duchess, author.
Title: Why news matters / by Duchess Harris.
Description: Minneapolis, Minnesota : Abdo Publishing, 2018. | Series: News literacy | Includes online resources and index.
Identifiers: LCCN 2017947121 | ISBN 9781532113918 (lib.bdg.) | ISBN 9781532152795 (ebook)
Subjects: LCSH: Mass media and public opinion--Juvenile literature. | American newspapers--History--Juvenile literature. | Values--Juvenile literature.
Classification: DDC 301.16--dc23
LC record available at https://lccn.loc.gov/2017947121

CONTENTS

CHAPTER
ONE

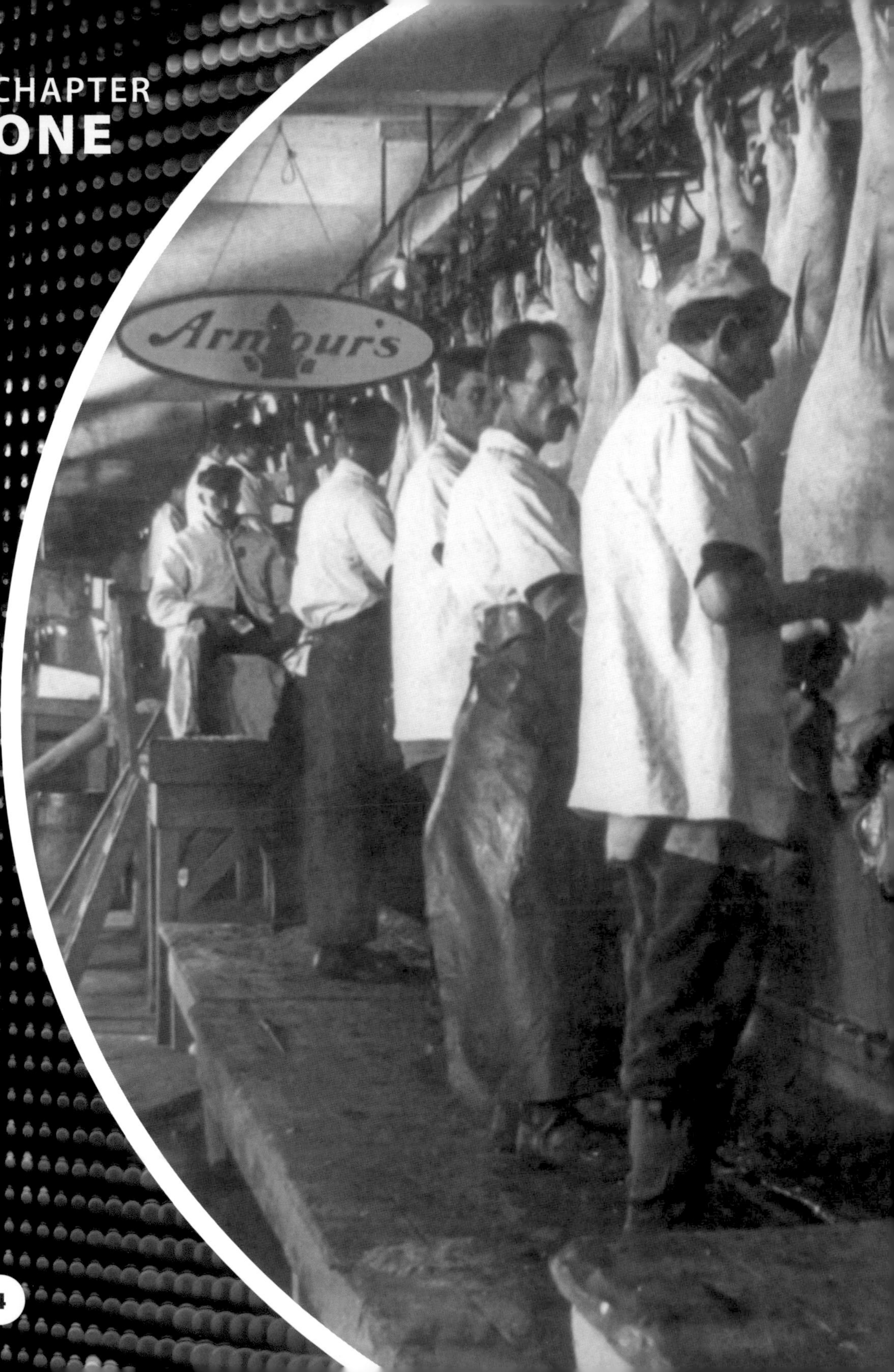

THE POWER OF ONE NEWS STORY

In the early 1900s, Chicago, Illinois, was the center of the meat processing industry. One part of the city came to be known as Packingtown. As many as 12 million hogs and beef cattle were processed there each year.

Many workers were poor immigrants. Women and children as young as 14 years old worked there, too. Life in Packingtown was hard. The working conditions were terrible, even dangerous. Employees worked in dark and stuffy rooms that were stiflingly hot in summer and freezing cold in winter. Many were

Meatpackers prepare hog carcasses for processing at Armour's Packing Plant in Chicago in 1909.

scheduled to work ten hours a day, six days a week. They worked on floors covered with animal blood, meat scraps, and dirty water. Sometimes the skin on their hands was eaten away by acid. Others lost fingers in the machines. Most of the workers earned only a few pennies per hour. Some workers died.

Horrible working conditions were not the only problem. Meat was piled on the floor before it was processed. It got scooped off the floor along with sawdust, rat droppings, rat poison, dead rats, and human saliva. Then it was packaged and sold to consumers. The Packingtown companies made employees work at night. They did not want meat inspectors to see them using diseased and rotten meats. Food that should have been thrown away was instead injected with chemicals. Then it was processed into cans and packages that were not properly labeled.

In 1904 workers went on strike to demand better working conditions and wages. The Packingtown companies brought in replacement workers. Those who continued to strike fell into poverty and debt. It seemed impossible to force the businesses to change their practices.

ENTER SINCLAIR

Then the editor of a newspaper called *Appeal to Reason* asked writer Upton Sinclair to investigate. Sinclair spent seven weeks in Chicago. The owners of the meatpacking plants had no idea who

IN THE REAL WORLD
THE NEED FOR JOURNALISTS

President Theodore Roosevelt said, "There should be relentless exposure of and attack on every evil man, whether politician or business man, every evil practice, whether in politics, business, or social life." He knew that there would be unethical people who would do harm to others for their own gain. With this statement, he pointed out that the best way to stop unethical people was for other people to expose them. This is the main role of investigative journalists. They uncover bad and often dangerous practices and help stop them.

Sinclair was. He was able to observe first-hand the dangerous conditions and practices.

When his investigation was complete, Sinclair wrote a book called *The Jungle.* Parts of it were released in multiple issues of *Appeal to Reason* in 1905. Then it was published as a book in 1906. *The Jungle* was a fictionalized but graphic view of what Sinclair had seen in Packingtown. He told readers about the bad working conditions and tainted meat products.

The Jungle became a best seller. Readers were horrified and angry. Sales of meat dropped. People demanded that the federal government take action. President Theodore Roosevelt put together a special commission to investigate Packingtown. The commission was able to prove that what Sinclair had written was true.

Upton Sinclair's book led to significant changes in the meatpacking industry.

THE JUNGLE

UPTON SINCLAIR

JOURNALISTS HELP GOVERNMENT WORKERS

When *The Jungle* was released, it made many people angry. One of these was Harvey Washington Wiley. Wiley worked for the US Department of Agriculture. He had been trying to secure government protection for consumers for many years. Sinclair's book gave him the evidence he needed to speed up the process. Wiley brought it to President Theodore Roosevelt, who agreed that it was time to take action.

FORCING ACTION

After the investigation, Congress worked quickly to address the situation. It passed two laws in 1906. One increased federal regulation and inspection of meatpacking. The other regulated how packages were labeled. It made it illegal to mislead consumers on labels. That law eventually led to the formation of the Food and Drug Administration. Meatpacking companies fought these laws, but they lost.

Employees at modern meatpacking plants work in much more sanitary conditions.

As a result, meat products became safer. Consumers began buying meat again. But it wasn't until the 1930s that employee safety became a government concern. In 1935 Congress passed a law making it legal for unions to form and bargain with employers in that industry.

Upton Sinclair spent just seven weeks in Packingtown. But he caused an entire industry to change its practices. He provided an early example of the power that the press has to change society for the better. Sinclair demonstrated why news matters.

STRAIGHT TO THE
SOURCE

Sinclair wanted readers to understand how badly workers were treated in the meatpacking plants. But journalist Karen Olsson notes that many readers focused on the poor quality of the food produced instead.

> *With the novel's publication, Sinclair achieved one of his goals:* The Jungle *was wildly successful. He failed to get his point across, though. 'I aimed at the public's heart,' Sinclair famously complained after the book was published, 'and by accident I hit it in the stomach.' Shocked by his lurid descriptions of what went on inside the factories, his readers were more worried about the possibility that there might be rats in their sausage than about the plight of the immigrant laborer. . . . That misreading was partly attributable to Sinclair's readers; then, as now, it's much easier to interest people in contaminated hamburgers than in injured workers.*

Source: Karen Olsson. "Welcome to the Jungle." *Slate*. The Slate Group, July 10, 2006. Web. Accessed May 5, 2017.

What's the Big Idea?

Read this text carefully. Determine its main idea. Then explain how the main idea is supported by details. Be sure to name at least two or three of those details.

CHAPTER
TWO

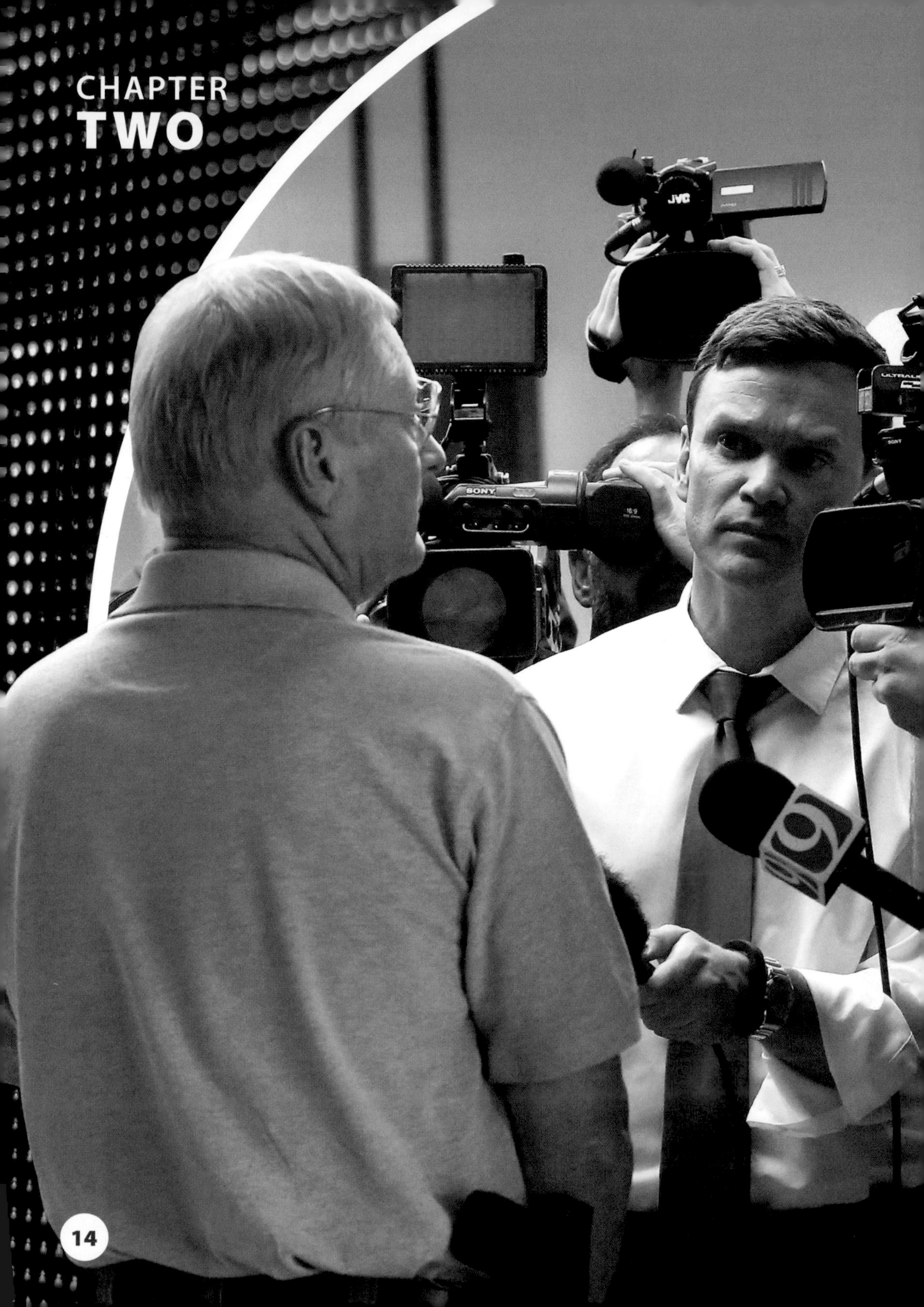

WHAT IS THE NEWS?

There are different kinds of news. But all news has the same basic goal: To inform readers. People need to know many types of information. That's why there are many different ways of covering the news.

TYPES OF NEWS

General news is covered at the national and international levels. Those stories report events that are of interest to people in many places. Other reporters cover things that are of interest only to people in a specific area or town.

When reporters do a great deal of research and investigating, they are doing

Reporters interview a subject outside a courtroom.

investigative journalism. The goal of this reporting is to uncover information that others want to stay hidden. They often expose practices that are unethical or harmful to the public.

OTHER KINDS OF NEWS

Another aspect of the news is opinion. An opinion is not necessarily based on fact. It is a reaction to something else. An opinion can lead to discussions that help people understand the issues. It can also lead to solutions.

WHERE PEOPLE GET NEWS

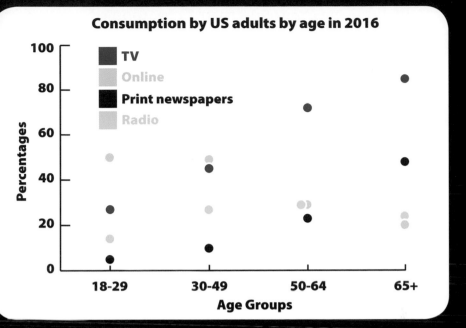

Consumption by US adults by age in 2016

- TV
- Online
- **Print newspapers**
- Radio

Percentages / Age Groups: 18-29, 30-49, 50-64, 65+

People get their news from different places. What are some of the different ways people get news? How does it vary according to age?

NEWS OUTLETS

Years ago, newspapers were the only medium that delivered news. Depending on where people lived, they might not get the news for days or even weeks. Newspapers were printed in cities. They were meant for local residents. Sometimes people shared the news in letters to family or friends. Those letters were sent by horse or by train. That could take a long time.

Technology improved over time. One of the biggest advances was the invention of the telegraph in 1844. Instead of taking days or weeks to send news, it was delivered by a telegraph wire. That meant that news could easily be transmitted all over the country. Newspapers anywhere could have access to national news. Reporters could also visit remote areas and send stories back to the newspapers much more easily. This became very important during the American Civil War (1861–1865). People learned what was happening in the war much sooner than before.

The next big advance was radio. After the telegraph was created, the search began for a way to transmit voices. By the late 1800s, different ways of sending voices were being studied. By 1910 radio was born. People who had a radio could listen to the news as it was being reported. Just as telegraphs helped inform people about the Civil War, radio helped inform people about World War I (1914–1918) and World War II (1939–1945).

As television gained popularity, viewers could watch news events such as the 1960 presidential debate between John F. Kennedy and Richard M. Nixon from their living rooms.

Television was the next major step. It was introduced to the public by manufacturer RCA in 1939. Television stations began offering news programs in the late 1940s. News consumers also caught up on current events at the movies. Newsreels ran before the main feature, showing the audience important events happening around the world.

The arrival of the Internet changed news again. Today people can find news stories around the clock. News outlets have multiple ways to share the news. They may publish a newspaper, host a website, and send e-mails to subscribers that feature links to their content. They may have a radio program, a website, and podcasts. Sometimes

WHY NEWSPAPERS STILL MATTER

Even with the ease of watching television and the speed of finding news on the Internet, newspapers still matter. Digital sources provide coverage of all the big stories. They can present that information almost immediately. But Web-only outlets are not as likely to cover smaller stories. They may not have enough staff to cover those stories either. Newspapers today have websites as well as print versions. They can provide news as it is happening via social media or their websites. In their print versions, they can do more in-depth reporting and fill out details of stories.

journalists from one type of news appear in another form. For example, a writer for a newspaper may appear on a TV news program or radio show.

FURTHER EVIDENCE

Chapter Two discusses the types of news that people consume. Opinion and editorial pages are part of news coverage. Visit the website below and read about editorial journalism. Find a quote that explains how you determine fact from opinion. Does this help you understand the difference between the two?

READING PRIMARY SOURCES: NEWSPAPER EDITORIALS
abducorelibrary.com/why-news-matters

CHAPTER
THREE

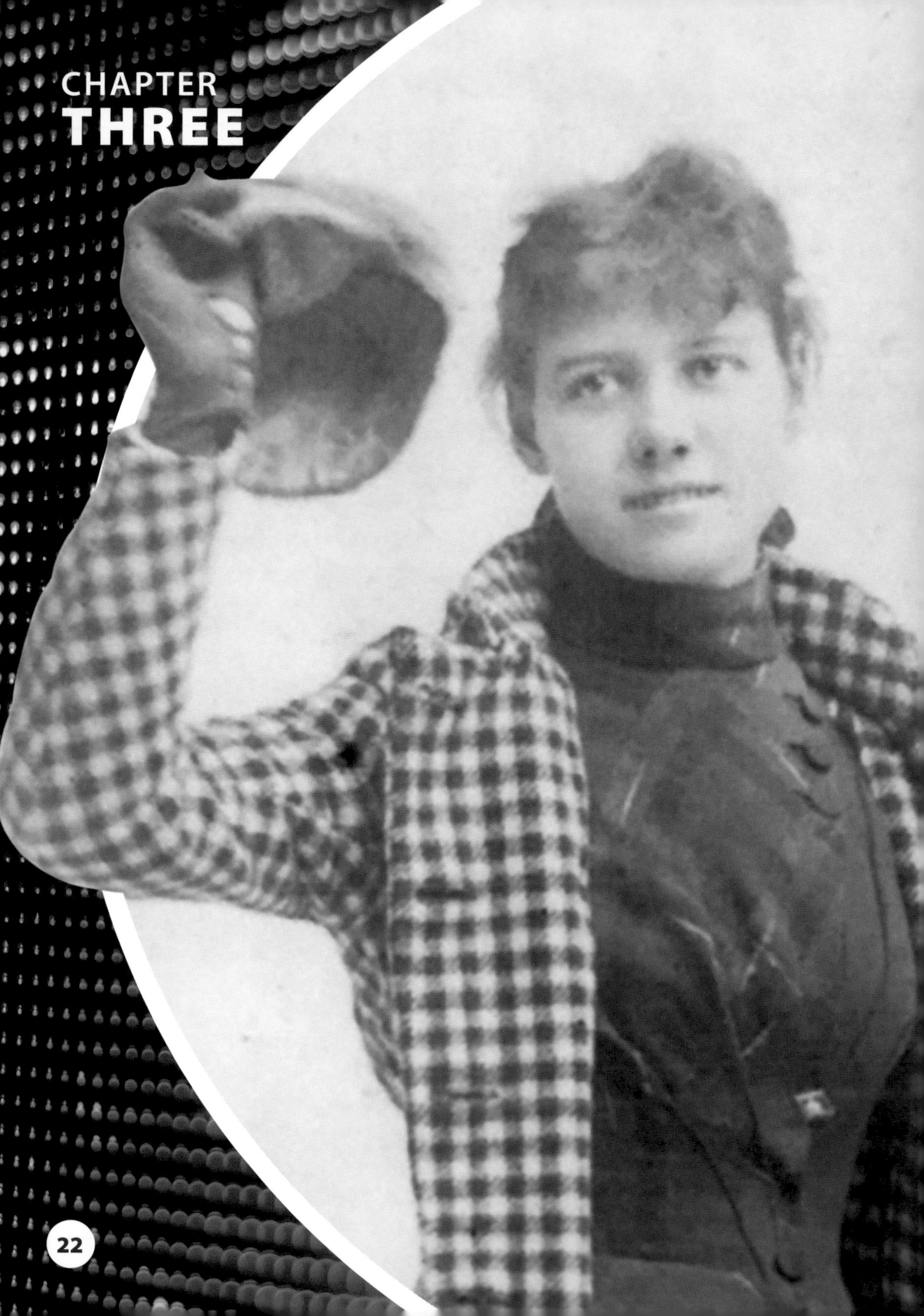

PIONEERING REPORTERS

Upton Sinclair was not the first person to make a difference by reporting the news. He was not the last either. Many people have helped change the world by reporting the news.

NELLIE BLY AND BLACKWELL'S ISLAND

Nellie Bly knew at a young age that she wanted to be a reporter. This was a hard thing for a woman to do in the late 1800s. She worked for a newspaper in Pittsburgh, Pennsylvania. But she was frustrated. Her assignments focused on softer topics such as fashion. She wanted to work on hard news.

Nellie Bly was a pioneer in the field of investigative journalism.

In 1887 she went to New York City. She wanted to work for the *New York World*. They said they would hire her if she was willing to do something dangerous. They wanted her to go undercover in a mental hospital to see how patients were treated.

YELLOW JOURNALISM

In the late 1800s, the term *yellow journalism* was popular. It described newspaper stories that were sensational and written to grab the reader's attention. It was not meant as a compliment. It began in New York City, where two newspaper owners competed to get the most readers. Joseph Pulitzer and William Randolph Hearst each tried to print the most eye-catching stories. To do that, at times they placed sensationalized details above the need to report truth.

In New York, people with mental illness were sent to an asylum on Blackwell's Island for treatment. But the treatments they received did not cure them. Bly pretended to have a mental illness. She was taken to the hospital and stayed ten days. While there, she witnessed many terrible things. Patients were beaten.

They were given ice-cold baths. People were forced to eat against their will or were starved. The food was sometimes rotten.

Her story was published in the *New York World* in 1887. It was published as a book the same year. Public officials in New York followed up by investigating and making sure patients were treated more humanely and safely. Bly went on to uncover more corruption in jails, factories, and even governments.

IDA TARBELL AND STANDARD OIL

Ida Tarbell was a teacher and writer. She was also one of the first writers to be called a muckraker. A muckraker is a journalist who digs deep and uncovers information that people in power might prefer stay hidden.

Tarbell's father was in the oil business. That industry was dominated by Standard Oil Company, owned by John D. Rockefeller. Rockefeller used unethical tactics to drive other oil companies out of business. That included bribing railroad officials to increase charges for other

oil companies. Then he would take over the territory. He became very wealthy doing this.

Tarbell began investigating Rockefeller's business practices in 1900. She found people in his company who were willing to speak with her. In 1902 she began writing a series of 19 articles about Standard Oil. *McClure's Magazine* published

A political cartoon depicts Standard Oil as a monster wrapping its tentacles around banks, small businesses, the railroads, and the government.

Ida Tarbell's reporting uncovered corruption in the oil industry.

her articles. They were later compiled into a book and released in 1904.

From Tarbell's writings, the public learned that Rockefeller was unethical. He formed a trust to dominate the oil business. A trust is an organization formed by several businesses to control prices and the market for goods. "Antitrust" means fighting unlawful actions that skew the competitive balance of an industry. When one business dominates an industry, it can charge any price it wants. That is not good for consumers.

Tarbell's work led to a US Supreme Court ruling against Standard Oil in 1911. The Court held that the company had violated the Sherman Antitrust Act. Standard Oil had to be broken down into smaller units that did business separately. That created fair competition in the marketplace.

EXPLORE ONLINE

Nellie Bly is famous for her work in the mental hospital. But she investigated many other things too. Read more about her investigations on the website below. Why were these important topics?

NATIONAL WOMEN'S HISTORY MUSEUM: NELLIE BLY
abdocorelibrary.com/why-news-matters

CHAPTER FOUR

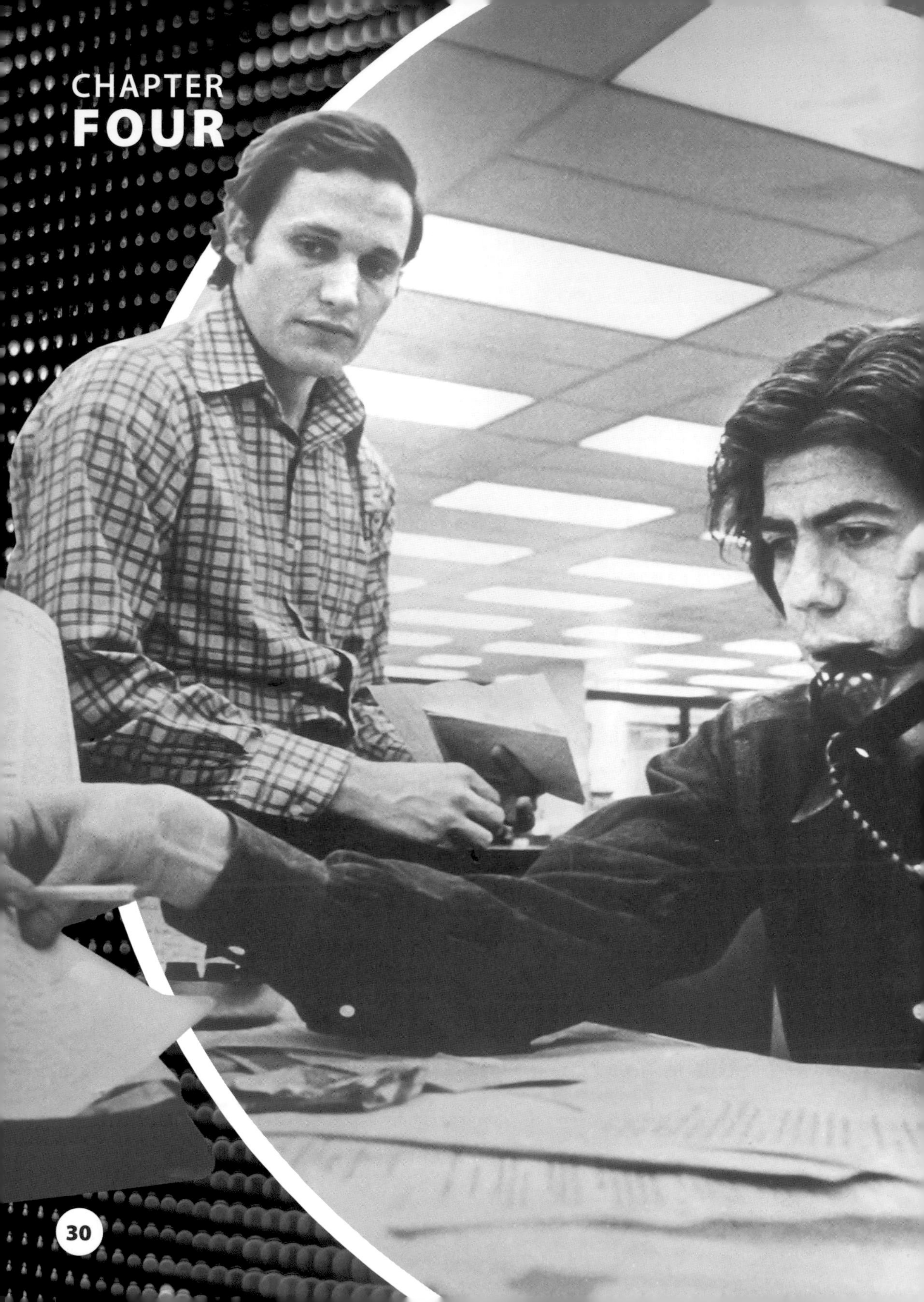

SEARCHING FOR TRUTH TODAY

Today's reporters benefit from improved technology. They can use the Internet to track down information and sources much more quickly. And just like Nellie Bly and Ida Tarbell, they are still uncovering big stories that some people would prefer remain hidden.

WOODWARD, BERNSTEIN, AND WATERGATE

In 1972 a short article in the *Washington Post* changed history. It noted that burglars had

Bob Woodward, *left*, and Carl Bernstein won a Pulitzer Prize for their coverage of the Watergate scandal in the *Washington Post*.

OTHER IMPORTANT NEWS

There are many other examples of reporters who uncovered important stories. In the 1950s, Senator Joseph McCarthy claimed there were more than 200 Communists working in the US government. Murrey Marder researched McCarthy's claims and proved they were false.

In the 1960s the war in Vietnam was not going as well as politicians said it was. David Halberstam's reporting on the war was credited with turning the American people against the war.

In 1968 a group of US soldiers murdered hundreds of innocent villagers in My Lai, Vietnam. The military tried to cover it up. Journalist Seymour Hersh made the story public, and the guilty troops were brought to justice.

been arrested at the Watergate building in Washington, DC. But this was no ordinary burglary. They had broken into the office of the Democratic National Committee. One of the burglars was an employee of President Richard Nixon's reelection campaign. The Democrats were opposing Nixon in the election.

Post reporters Bob Woodward and Carl Bernstein investigated why a political staffer would be involved in a burglary. What they discovered led to one of the biggest political scandals in American history. They found evidence that Nixon and several other Republicans were aware of the break-in. Some of Nixon's aides were found to have actively planned it. They only wanted it to look like a burglary. The main goal of the break-in was to place hidden microphones in the offices so Nixon's campaign could listen to the Democrats' plans. Then they tried to cover up their actions.

Republicans tried to shut down the investigation. But Woodward and Bernstein kept digging. They found more connections between Nixon's staff and the burglary. By 1974 public outcry against Nixon was strong. Many wanted him to be impeached. That is the process of removing a president from office for wrongdoing. Instead of going through the impeachment process, Nixon chose to resign. He was the first US president ever to resign from office.

Nixon Resigns

By Carroll Kilpatrick

Ford Assumes Presidency Today

By Jules Witcover

Era of Good Feeling
Congress Expects Harmony

By Spencer Rich and Richard L. Lyons

A Solemn Change
Power Is Passed Quietly

By Richard Harwood and Haynes Johnson

The front page of the *Washington Post* on August 8, 1974

NSA SURVEILLANCE

The National Security Agency (NSA) collects information

on matters of national security. This is done to help

NEW TECHNOLOGY, NEW NEWS SOURCES

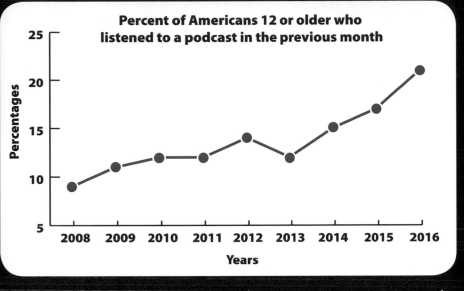

Percent of Americans 12 or older who listened to a podcast in the previous month

People might not be relying on radio as a news source as much as they once did. But that doesn't mean they're not listening to the news. Podcasts have quickly grown in popularity, and many of the most downloaded podcasts cover news and related topics.

prevent terrorism and other threats against the country. In 2013 a former intelligence employee named Edward Snowden leaked several NSA documents. They showed that the NSA was collecting phone records from thousands of American citizens. The NSA gathered this information even on people who had no criminal history and were not under suspicion.

Newspapers such as the *Washington Post* and the *Guardian* began researching. They found that the NSA was also collecting Internet records from Americans. Further investigation found that the NSA had broken privacy rules many times. It had also collected millions of e-mail addresses, as well as location information from smartphones.

Even worse, the NSA had been spying on foreign leaders who were US allies. This surveillance was done without the knowledge and permission of Congress. When it came out, the foreign leaders were very angry.

In 2015 a federal appeals court found that the NSA surveillance was illegal. Government committees reviewed the NSA surveillance programs. Changes were made to protect the privacy of Americans who are not suspected of committing crimes.

Former NSA employee Edward Snowden has been an outspoken critic of illegal surveillance.

Demonstrators protest the NSA surveillance program in Washington, DC, in 2013.

STUDENT JOURNALISTS AND THE SCHOOL PRINCIPAL

In 2017 students at Pittsburg High School in Kansas decided to research their new principal for the school newspaper. They were surprised by what they found. The principal said she had received a degree from the University of Tulsa. But the university there had no

record of her. The principal said she had gotten her advanced college degrees from Corllins University. When the students researched that, they found it was not an accredited university. That meant it was not approved by the US Department of Education. It also meant the principal had not told the truth about her background and was not qualified for the job. After the

STICKING WITH IT

The Kansas students who investigated their principal were not supported by everyone in their community. Gina Mathew, one of the six reporters who led the paper's investigation, noted that some people thought they should ignore the discrepancies. But Mathew said, "Those inconsistencies were what needed to be presented within our own newspaper, and to highlight to the community what we had found. . . . We knew that there was a story to be heard here, and that's exactly what our paper sought out to do." This is the same mind-set the early muckrakers had.

students' research was made public, the principal resigned.

These students were following the tradition established by many inquisitive and persistent journalists before them. Whether it be Upton Sinclair's Chicago meatpacking plants or a high school in Kansas, the United States has a rich history of investigative journalism that reports difficult truths and holds powerful people to account for their actions.

STRAIGHT TO THE
SOURCE

How important is freedom of the press today? One Constitutional watchdog says there is more reason than ever to protect this right.

The rise of the national security state and the proliferation of new surveillance technologies have created new challenges to media freedom. The government has launched an unprecedented crackdown on whistleblowers, targeting journalists in order to find their sources. Whistleblowers face prosecution under the World War One-era Espionage Act for leaks to the press in the public interest. And in the face of a growing surveillance apparatus, journalists must go to new lengths to protect sources and, by extension, the public's right to know.

Source: "Freedom of the Press." *The American Civil Liberties Union*. www.aclu.org, n.d. Web. Accessed July 20, 2017.

Changing Minds

Take a position on whether whistleblowers should be punished for leaking classified information. Then imagine that your best friend has the opposite opinion. Write a short essay trying to change your friend's mind. Make sure you detail your opinion and your reason for it. Include facts and details that support your reasons.

FAST FACTS

- Upton Sinclair investigated the conditions at Chicago meatpacking plants. He learned many awful things. He then wrote about them so the public would know the truth. Because of his writing, laws were passed to make meatpacking safer for workers and for consumers.

- There are different kinds of news: investigative, international/national, regional/local, opinion, and entertainment. These have different roles, but all should be based on facts.

- There are also different ways to find the news. Today you can find news in print sources such as newspapers and magazines, on television and radio, and on the Internet.

- Many reporters have presented terrible things in the news. Nellie Bly exposed a mental hospital that treated patients cruelly. Ida Tarbell wrote about how Standard Oil used unethical tactics to drive competitors out of business. Bob Woodward and Carl Bernstein uncovered corruption in the White House. Students in Kansas discovered that their new principal did not have the necessary credentials to be a principal. In each case, changes were made in response to these reports.

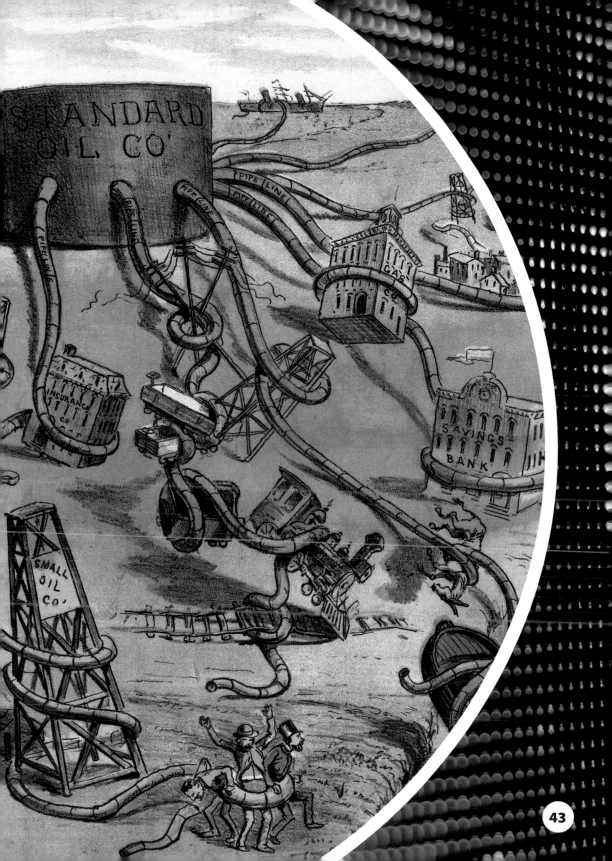

STOP AND
THINK

Tell the Tale

Chapter One talks about conditions in meatpacking plants. Write 200 words as if you were a reporter at the plant. What do you see? How do you feel?

Surprise Me

Chapter Two talks about different types of news outlets. Write a few sentences about the two or three ideas you found most surprising. What surprised you about each?

Dig Deeper

What questions do you still have about why news matters? With an adult's help, find a few reliable sources to answer your questions. Write a paragraph about what you learned.

Say What?

Studying the news can mean learning a lot of new vocabulary. Find five words in this book you have never heard before. Use a dictionary to find out what they mean. Then write the meanings in your own words, and use each word in a new sentence.

GLOSSARY

accredited
officially recognized by a
regulatory group

antitrust
preventing one company or
organization from controlling
all business in its field

asylum
an outdated term for a
hospital that treats people
suffering from mental illness

commission
a group of people in
government who have a
specific task or focus

investigate
to examine and research in
close detail

journalism
researching, writing,
editing, and reporting
the news

muckraker
an old-fashioned term
for a journalist who
uncovers scandals

strike
a work stoppage organized
to force employers to give in
to demands by workers

unethical
not moral or well-behaved

union
a group of workers who
organize to protect
their rights

ONLINE RESOURCES

To learn more about why news matters, visit our free resource websites below.

Visit **abdocorelibrary.com** for free Common Core resources for teachers and students, including vetted activities, multimedia, and booklinks, for deeper subject comprehension.

Visit **abdobooklinks.com** for free additional online weblinks for further learning. These links are routinely monitored and updated to provide the most current information available.

LEARN MORE

Mahoney, Ellen Voelckers. *Nellie Bly and Investigative Journalism for Kids: Mighty Muckrakers from the Golden Age to Today, with 21 Activities.* Chicago, IL: Chicago Review Press, 2015.

ABOUT THE
AUTHOR

Duchess Harris, JD, PhD

Professor Harris is the chair of the American Studies Department at Macalester College. The author and coauthor of four books (*Hidden Human Computers: The Black Women of NASA* and *Black Lives Matter* with Sue Bradford Edwards, *Racially Writing the Republic: Racists, Race Rebels, and Transformations of American Identity* with Bruce Baum, and *Black Feminist Politics from Kennedy to Clinton/Obama*), she has been an associate editor for *Litigation News*, the American Bar Association Section's quarterly flagship publication, and was the first editor-in-chief of *Law Raza Journal*, an interactive online race and the law journal for William Mitchell College of Law.

She has earned a PhD in American Studies from the University of Minnesota and a Juris Doctorate from William Mitchell College of Law.

INDEX